The Water Poems

Sylvia Cavanaugh, Nancy Harrison Durdin, Dawn Hogue, Maryann Hurtt, Georgia Ressmeyer, & Marilyn Zelke Windau

The Grand Avenue Poetry Collective

Sheboygan, Wisconsin | Tucson, Arizona

The Water Poems

Water's Edge Press LLC
Tucson, Arizona
watersedgepress.com

© 2017, 2023 by Water's Edge Press LLC

All rights reserved. This book or any portion thereof may not be reproduced or used in any manner whatsoever without the express written permission of the publisher except for the use of brief quotations in a book review.

Published 2023

First Edition published 2017
Second Edition published 2023
Printed in the United States of America

ISBN: 978-1-952526-14-5

Credits:
Original cover photography by Jeff Hutchison, used with permission.
Book design by Water's Edge Press
Haiku on secion divider pages by Dawn Hogue

Also by The Grand Avenue Poetry Collective

The Aging Poems

One

Pristine Joy 1

Water 2

In Balance 3

Daedalus Surfs Refugio Beach 4

Door County Cove 5

Homecoming 6

Of Poems 7

I Get Up 8

Comfort 9

No Words 10

On the Beach at Daybreak 11

Great Lake Lullaby 12

Contemplating Eternity at River's Edge 13

Missoula Night 14

Water Aria 15

Rope Climb 16

Last Sail 18

Two

Icarus Was My Brother 21

Deliciously Cold 22

Summer at Riverview Middle School 23

Beach Glass 24

Water Looking Up 25

Lake Michigan Shoreline 26

To Life! 27

Crossing the River at Leesburg 28

The Big Fish 29

Mary 30

Midsummer, 1961 31

A Block Away Tradition 32

Nineteen-Fifties Vacation 33

Streamwise 34

Dance of the Pigeon River 35

Day Begins 36

The Bundled Trundler 37

Three

I Need a Storm 41

Honeymoon Cottage in Cedar Key 42

Mermaid Tattoo Becomes Enmeshed in Her Relationship 43

Sky View 44

Down by the Riverside 45

Summer Storm 46

Sea Levels Rising 47

Back to "Mothers' Waters" 48

The river is insulted 49

The River's Rising and Other Important Things 50

Alligator Log 51

My Repugnant Tar Creek Orange Self 52

Rain on a Tuesday Afternoon Amidst a Drought 53

Sheboygan Marsh 6 a.m. 54

Water When the Wind Blows 55

Bergie Bits 56

Existential Rain 57

There Was This Original Me 58

The Opportunist 59

Naucrate 60

Four

In Memoriam 63

every poem 64

Ahab and the Whale 65

Evening Comes to Vernazza 66

Beach Picnic 67

Water Wolf 68

I Dream in Water 69

Deer on the Kohler Andrae Crestline 70

Empty Nest 71

Candle Waxes — Love Wanes 72

On the Menu 73

River Mistress 74

Letter to Lorine 75

Trinity 76

Dragonflies 77

River in the Sea 78

Cottage Summer 79

How Nancy Drew Learned to Fish 80

One

*Water flows onward.
Leaves are boats under blue skies.
Herons nest in shade.*

Pristine Joy

Slowly, slowly Lake Michigan opens
her palms and scatters shimmers.

Sheets of water spread like salve
across the pockmarked backs
of sandbars close to shore, smoothing
gouges made by coarser waves
before collecting in ponds
around my toes.

Ring-billed gulls, grasses, poplars,
dunes, and I receive Lake's gifts
with dew still silvering our wings
and hair.

Lake's beauty, needing to be shared,
cries out for dragonflies and monarchs,
swallows, sanderlings to join our
early-morning fling at pristine joy.

The day is new, our hearts still pure,
and sparkling light surrounds us.

Georgia Ressmeyer

Water

So thin.
It runs through my fingers
like sateen ribbon,
waves of blue,
with little white loops
at its edges.
They call it bouclé
when it's curl-spun,
when it's foam.

Transparent,
when poured into a glass,
a clear beaker.
I would drink it turquoise,
or olive green, iron red,
fluorescent orange—
its disguises when I look away,
a ways out from bow to horizon.

Loud, the crashing.
Soft, the lapping.
Silent as air, insistent as breathing.

Marilyn Zelke Windau

In Balance

from the art quilt "In Balance" by Lindi Kuritz

The azure sea laps lightly upon this beach
where I press with deliberation my feet,
each toe into the sand, wet and cool,
ready for evening.

This is the place where fishermen gathered
fallen rocks, round as their wives' full bellies
or flat as planed planks, and balanced them
as sentry towers or in Iris's honor to welcome
them home, Zephryus billowing their sails
gently into shore.

I begin with one small, smooth granite stone,
closing first my fingers over it as it cools my palm
and set it as my base. Upon it I set a nearby ovoid,
milky as an opal. A bullet shaped stone is next.
Its black and white speckled shell teeters a moment
before settling into harmony. For the top a pebble
the color of morning, and I find for it a niche
to nestle in.

So it stands
until I must leave it,
small and unprotected from a wave's rush
or the menace of children or the unknowing step
of another, who may bend, and find,
as I did, the makings of balance.

Dawn Hogue

Daedalus Surfs Refugio Beach

I saw him there
gray hair and spine
soldiered stiff
but with nimble ankles
to work the board
this is how he flies now
skimming the rising breast
of the sea
he glides the high tide
rides the moon goddess
in the full sun of morning
the sea permitting the light
to penetrate only the high
vaulting arc of the wave
blue giving way to beryl

but mostly the sea casts off the sun
in a scattering of sharp sparkle
like a shriek
of triumphant laughter

and when the wave he rides
is almost spent
and the board careens one way
and he the other
sideways or backwards
he washes up
in the sizzle of white foam
not quite water
not quite air

he thinks he once knew
free love
given and taken
in patchouli moonglo rooms
thinks he knew his way
around the maze
now he kisses the sand
and salt
refugio,
O, refugio

Sylvia Cavanaugh

Door County Cove

The path takes turns with the trees.
Sometimes the trees win.
The path curves to allow them their victory.
Sometimes the path carves a straight line
and the trees bend in homage.
Up a small incline the forest abruptly relinquishes its guard.
A wide beach of white smooth stones, a sheltered cove,
old pilings from a long gone wharf and water, steel gray-blue water.
Calm. No wake. Now wave. No white cap.
In the distance, floating seemingly weightless,
eleven white swans are visible in sunlight,
only when in profile.
Turning, they're gone. Turning, they're majestic.
Their curved necks own the lake's cove.
Overhead gliding, wing-dip slanting, more aerial relatives fly by,
low, looking for hospitality.
They land at an unpretentious distance, paddle feet slowly,
wait for acceptance.
Low honking, honking, from already residents voice invitation.
Newcomers join in reunion.

Marilyn Zelke Windau

Homecoming

may we be river smooth stones
in snow cold water
waiting for the return
of our salmon brothers and sisters

coontail algae
wave their fronds
and we will lie solemn
with respect

the black bears are simply hungry, maybe greedy
and that old man on the gravel bank
knows soon it will be
his turn

Maryann Hurtt

Of Poems

poems are bread and water
fire and rusty steel
clouds and bird wings
in the sky...
beating out a rhythm
in essential form

Nancy Harrison Durdin

I Get Up

"Down at the edge, round by the corner
Close to the end, down by a river
Seasons will pass you by
I get up, I get down"

From "Close to the Edge" by Yes

The path slopes down
to the river bank. At
my approach, the
nesting geese edge
their way round
each other by
twos and threes to the water, the
babies safe at their corner.
I long to see up close
a monarch flitting to
un-mowed milkweed, the
prairie flowers at path's end,
bright until sun is down,
but now I sit for a moment by
the cool stillness, a cloud casting a
shady canopy over this river,
which, at all seasons
has its own will.
I never pass
this way without thinking of you
or of how lucky I am to be here by
this solitude, this peace. I
want you to know that each day I get
up, each morning I get up
and think of you, and I
know what is left to me. I get
up, and I will not easily lie down.

Dawn Hogue

Comfort

In ascending,
the white of gull wingcut
through horizontal stripes of lake.
Steel blue, Payne's grey,
obsidian, and navy layers
painted the water to sky's line.
Wisconsin sand,
Wisconsin bird eyes sought
Michigan shores,
believed in the unseen.
Soft, the lapping of waves
drew ribbon line scallops on sand.
Bubblefoam rhythm-popped
on smooth, wet pebbles.
The gull bent wings,
feather flew, settle-floated
in the ease of comfort.

Marilyn Zelke Windau

No Words

grief stricken
at the funeral
our fierce embrace
your tears running
down my cheek
both of us silent
no words needed

Nancy Harrison Durdin

On the Beach at Daybreak

Who will share the day's
first magic with you:

project gold coins onto your
retinas, glue a mystery twin

to the swing of your arms,
brace a shining goblet

on the lake for you to drink
fading purple shadows from?

No tangible body—
no skin, no bones, no flesh—

but just as warm as any you
might hug at home.

Take the cup that's offered
on a sparkling tray.

Here is the gift of one cool sip:
another flawless day.

Georgia Ressmeyer

Great Lake Lullaby

his fox tail shadow
blurs into breathe-green woods
spider webs tickle the air
absorb the sound
of his bark
alewives glitter the beach
and the Lake
pushes and pulls
pushes and pulls

tonight
I will close my eyes
listen deep
hear divine heart beat
in everything

lullaby and good night

Maryann Hurtt

Contemplating Eternity at River's Edge

"Souls of Poets dead and gone,
What Elysium have ye known,
Happy field or mossy cavern,
Choicer than the Mermaid Tavern?"

From "Lines on the Mermaid Tavern" by John Keats

On this mossy bank I think of souls
long gone and wonder where their sense of
self resides. Are they among the ancient poets
in Dante's green limbo, elevated among the dead,
robed in pure white, their oiled and
sandaled feet walking easily, life's pain long gone?

Could I ask "What
is heaven?" They might say "To imagine Elysium
is to have
such hope and peace that ye
in life have never known."

Could I ask, "Are you now happy?"
in a poppy field
fragrant with frankincense or
lavender or sage, rank and mossy,
at the edges of a river cavern.

They might reply, "In life no landscape could be choicer
than the one we live in now, far better than
your river's edge." And might they wink before joining the
others at their local pub, where the barmaid is a mermaid
at Hades' raucous tavern.

Dawn Hogue

Missoula Night

in this river town
I eat huckleberry ice cream
listen to tunes echo off water
but it's a city
and night sneaks its hood
over all of us
I walk the streets now
bright lights
overhead so different
from Clark Fork's cattails
mud and muck
where if I dawdle silent
a lone heron will stand vigil
and even water's sound
could place its arms
around me

Maryann Hurtt

Water Aria

She built her nest on the sanded shore
of a small northern Wisconsin lake
named Timm's.
She swam and preened,
sang her loon song in early morning,
when she thought no one could hear
her aria to the dawn and to her eggs.

She floated the water, hooded in black,
with the grace of a ballerina,
arching her neck in yoga-like movements,
her red eyes deciphering food
in the water's blueness.

Paddling toward shore, she stub-footed
her webbed feet to the sanctuary
of her children's home.

He was waiting there:
her mate, her husband of shared responsibility.
She relieved him of his care for hers.

Nestling down on those two eggs,
she warmed life,
awaited new voices,
their springtime opera in the north woods.

Marilyn Zelke Windau

Rope Climb

Sun-filtered woods with their hard packed trails
meander their steep slope to the river
where an arched railroad bridge casts sun-wrought shade
from hand hewn stones of hazy men

trains sear civilization's untamed wound
tied to rails they sway rough clank through named towns
found the boy in me, the one I waited to love

I hurtle past accusation as Elvis on the radio
pleads plaintive truth of suspicious minds like this
rasp of burn hazel and how the sharp smell of weeds
permeates the breath of July's cicada whir
straight down the spine of afternoon

I prefer the uncaring face of this river to that
of the universe with its galaxies
in the water's particulate waste I taste the metal
of my blood as I steel myself against its forward press
my privacy cradled and cool caressed
the river's dark indifference saturates my need

today I fly across a slumped summer waterfall
to grab tight this spent rope, limpid-hung expectant
from the stone bridge, shoulderer of trains that
halt my breath and shudder my thoughts

I muscle my way up the thick twist of hemp
entranced by its endless double twine of self-embrace
hand over hand the rope now taut above me
rough scrapes my thighs to the holding clasp of feet
beneath the strain of bone and tendon
its frayed end swings the heavy spin of infinity

tonight I will join the women who lean
back into folding chairs and intertwine their
stories on the front stoops of houses fused
together with interlocking bricks

frosted lips will form words while legs cross one
over the other with the absentminded turn of ankle
to guide the dangle of pink polished toes
as they trace the slow arc of doubt

Sylvia Cavanaugh

Last Sail

If Dad were still alive and working,
he'd be near the end of his vacation.
Each sailing jaunt would take on
extra poignancy.

All sense impressions—salt water's
taste and smell, the flutter and snap
of sails as we came about,
the burn of line running through palms
and fingers, shades of blue and silver
streaking water, sky—would be
rolled in sailcloth, carefully stowed.

No wonder Dad chose to die at the end
of July. The weather felt just right
for that last sail of his vacation—

and though he'd have to go alone,
it was easy for us to imagine the joy
he felt as the first breeze took him,
his over-the-shoulder smile
at those of us waving from shore,
then out to sea and the ultimate freedom.

Georgia Ressmeyer

Two

*Sunburned children shout,
zig-zagging feet on hot sand.
White gulls soar above the blue.*

Icarus Was My Brother

His love of vermillion
marked him
as my mad mother's favorite
a flavor affinity
between the two of them

a shared recklessness
seemed to string them together
strands of carnival lights
at the beach
on a hot summer's night

but their affinity
could be chilled, too
as in brilliant Twin Pop
perfection
like when the sun paints the sky
in colors of flame
as it cools into the horizon
of a hungry roiling sea

Sylvia Cavanaugh

Deliciously Cold

In the hottest part of summer,
we gymshoe, streamshoe slide
off wormy, algaed rocks.
The water of the south branch
of the Pemenebonwon is cold,
deliciously cold.

We make our way down
the slippery, over grassed path
to the clear, rock-filled water.
Armed with a round plastic basin,
a soap bar, and a golden retriever,
we descend, feeling our way to cool.

The dog jumps, floating tail
and back hair, pumping paws,
climbs onto the big rock,
accepts ownership of same,
shakes her glory.

We soap ourselves,
and the dog on the big rock.
We scoop and lift from below us
small rocks, throw them
to the dam we build,
deepening our dipping area.

Branches, limbs, flora debris are cleared
at this time of year.
Our plunge area is a beat this,
an I can submerge quicker challenge.

Cold in August is not the same
as cold in January.
It's a wanted, sought,
treasured relief.

Marilyn Zelke Windau

Summer at Riverview Middle School

It's recess for this gaggle
of summer school students
who head to the river
this bright July morning.
These gondola geese
float without passengers
upon sparkling ripples
near a burdock bank.
A frog croaks, a minnow flits,
and apart from their charges,
even the teachers are in no hurry
to head back to class as they
make their skim swoosh landing
near the opposite shore.

Dawn Hogue

Beach Glass

Hanging out on the beach
fingers sifting through sand
I uncover emerald green glass
with frosty patina
worn bottom of a bottle
no longer a circle
it whispers of silica
and the white hot flame
of its birth

while I mummer of carbon
how I began as a lumbering orb
hungry and beckoning
until I swallowed a fish
swallowed her whole
and drank from a river
of iron and air

the glass and I speak
of accidents and misjudgments
our edges made irregular and sharp
and the way men thought of us
as vessels
I attempt a joke about envy
but it comes across as awkward
so I confess the time I packed up and left

explain the way my son, as a child
always hurled himself
into this sweet water sea
even now
he gives himself over
to the grasp of waves
joins the tide of young men
adrift in the pungent inhale
the swirl and the swell

Sylvia Cavanaugh

Water Looking Up

Round brown stones splashed
  by the rushing water,
water warmed by the dappled sun,
    sun edited by the trees of leaves,
leaves dripping color,
    color in the moving water,
water making a gentle stew of things,
   things with primordial echoes,
echoes of the faces peering in.

Nancy Harrison Durdin

Lake Michigan Shoreline

after viewing Ray Hagerman's painting
"Lake Michigan Shoreline"

It's late September.
Sailboats race
the yacht club's fall,
forgiving course.
Summer antics are done,
gone south with Illinois sailors,
who came to trim their jibs
on these rural wind's paths.
West breezes blow warm air
over a cooler, standoffish lake.
Gulls float-doze,
meditate on rhythmic wave laps.

Yellowed grass stands tall, thin.
Stiff-brittle now, sharp to the touch,
it breaks off with a retirement growl
of saved up resistance.

Bare feet touch surprise.
They remember the burn, the heatdescending
sink, the skin-scorch to pink.
This granular sand cool pumices
rough edges of heel, of arch, of toe.
It allows the standing traveler
moments of ease, of reflection
in water and thought.

Lead grey lines the horizon.
Aqua softens forward distance.
White creped ridges sashay
their ruffles to the shoreline.
These colors hum-sing the lake,
tune the quiet, await future cold
with calm resignation.

Marilyn Zelke Windau

To Life!

To the glinting, noisy life of the Sheboygan River
as it winds toward Lake Michigan on a June morning

To swallows swooping, wheeling, almost skimming
the surface, scooping lake flies from the air

To swallow-nestlings under the boardwalk, squawking
to be fed as walkers tread the planks overhead

To juvenile ring-billed gulls flying in loops
over the water, squealing, chasing one another

To servers sliding wooden benches from tabletops
as outdoor seating for the coffee shop

To an old man and his scruffy black dog, whose nails
clack on the decking as they walk

To cars rattling the metal plates of the Eighth Street
drawbridge — drivers rushing to work

To the see-saw call of a killdeer pacing the wild edge
of a parking lot

To small children wheeled by parents, one child
babbling nonsense, the other quacking at a goose

To the lively chirps of sparrows as they mate or
fight in the grass

To the joys of the morning, the veiled orange sun,
cool breeze, glassy river

To Life! — and to all who chirp, quack, scrape,
walk, or talk. This is how we play ours out.

Georgia Ressmeyer

Crossing the River at Leesburg

the Potomac
when I was twelve
held me in watery arms
felt safe
yet I knew the pull
of north and south border
to cross you leave
behind

pieces of your self
fifty years later, I study war
men, young boys terrified
their brothers washed down river
the war so glorious
suddenly becomes the warmth of blood
mixed in these waters
drowning dreams
joining enemy and friend
into open then closed eye bond
gray and blue
make no difference
when it's your time to say
good-by
the water keeps flowing

Maryann Hurtt

The Big Fish

Scalloped puffs of clouds tiered the cerulean sky.
The lake was striped with steel grey and aqua.
On the breakwater three young fishermen
followed the iron wall watching
the big fish.
They were 14ish and united in their quest.
One, a chubby dropwaist blue jean boy,
his yellow polka-dotted jockey shorts clinging
to his bellyroll, released
a fistful of sand
in a stream to the water.
"I'll make him move toward you."
"Don't scare'm!"
the tall skinny one said.
Cubs towel wrapping
his shoulders, Cubs cap pulled
down tight to his ears in the lake wind,
he dropped his line in front
of the big fish.
The third, bare-chested, pale
in the early summer
sun, threw bait out
in front of the fish
but not out in front
of the hook, leading
him on, guiding
him to the capture.
All the way down to the end of the breakwater:
Walk, drop hook, throw bait.
Walk, drop hook, throw bait.
The fish with a snap
of his tail jolted
and swam towards the aqua
stripes of the horizon.

Marilyn Zelke Windau

Mary

Aren't you hot, Mary,
on this summer day,
under those layers of woven
baby blue and white you wear
as you stand watch over the cemetery?
Surely even your bare face
and outstretched hands
swelter in this heat.

Wouldn't you rather be wearing
a tank top and shorts, or at least
linen pants and a sleeveless cotton tunic.
That would set off your strappy sandals
so well. Instead you stand for eternity,
or as long as earth-life gives to
statues these days, in a cumbersome
habit, a burqa, of sorts, a covering
men invented to hide their own shame.

I imagine you under the moon,
stripped down to your dainties,
wandering barefoot in the cool grass,
tossing your wimple behind you
as you run toward the river,
lightness in your heart.

Dawn Hogue

Midsummer, 1961

Dostoevsky, Raskolnikov,
brain fever, write a letter,
walk barefoot up a dusty
road to mail it, laze
in a Guatemalan sling
strung between two oaks,
doze with a mildew-scented
book across my chest,
dream of writing classic
novels popular with fungi,
emerge from the hammock
as if from a chrysalis,
pull a damp swimsuit off
the line, wear it as skin,
run to the beach, drop
towel and book next to my
sisters' things, dive in,
dive in, the water's clean,
the chill bracing if I
keep my limbs churning,
swim as far as I can, then
float on my back, let the
sky show me how large
the world is, let the sea
hum with the sound of all
creatures breathing as one.

Georgia Ressmeyer

A Block Away Tradition

I used to go down to the lake
when I was a teenager.
I would place my bare feet
on the sand where alewives
lingered their bodies and stench.
I positioned my feet toward the flow,
daring the wave wash,
the foam curl,
the cold Lake Michigan water
to victimize my toes.
It won in June and July,
but August brought warm!
My toes wriggled,
stood up and cheered!
Toes advanced to feet,
feet to ankles,
ankles to knees,
and soon I was immersed,
raising ballet legs to the blue sky,
toes up but yearning to dive.

Marilyn Zelke Windau

Nineteen-Fifties Vacation

Kids in flip flops, our feet powdered with sand
and dust, ran up and down the slanting aisles
of the five-and-dime, itchy-palmed with coins
we couldn't wait to spend on pop-it beads,
baseball cards, beach-related toys.

A trip into town felt like a blitz. Dad made us
pick whether to be dropped off at the library
or the dime store, our choices of books
and baubles always impulsively made.

Dad on vacation couldn't wait to get back
to the cottage for a quick lunch, then out
on our sailboat, the Horsefly, even if
there wasn't a hiccup of wind.

Once out in the bay we might sit, limp of wind
and breath, waiting for a cat's-paw of a breeze
to steal over the water and nudge us ahead.

Usually the wind picked up within an hour. Then
we might scoot. We liked it best when the boat
heeled and bounced on the waves, the sea spray
refreshing us, investing us with daring.

Since that time, only our bodies have obsolesced—
not those happy memories, which are buffed
to a brighter shine with each reliving.

Maybe to die is just to float in a glittery pond
of happiest images from the past—
memories so sharp they leave no gaps for
thoughts of moving forward, or of turning back.

Georgia Ressmeyer

Streamwise

They're hungry—
the little fish.
They're greedy.
They race from side stream
to fast, over-rock water
to gulp the worm.
Some swallow so deeply,
they can't survive hook removal.

Children are like that.
They hunger with eyes
bigger than their stomach.
They want what they see.
They'll detour from need to want.
They love the shiny, the beckoning swivel
of spoon lure.

Let them go for the grasp.
Let them nibble, not gulp.
Let them get streamwise, streetwise.
Hope that they swim strongly against current
for a lifetime of discovery.

Marilyn Zelke Windau

Dance of the Pigeon River

My mother and I turned up
at Maywood nature center
with its lofty room and plate glass window
overlooking wild grasses
for a program called "Moving Field Guide"
led by a dance troupe from Maryland

we were outnumbered
of the twelve present
seven were dancers
and the program turned out to be
"choreographing nature into our lives"
my mother almost left over it

but the dancers would not be denied
we stumbled down the steep slope
to the Pigeon River
gliding its late April silver
as though it were the pool of Narcissus
but with eddies of booze
and nervous breakdown

my mother and I crouch and twirl
rising together from chill mud to sky
and, as if we were artists,
thumb for perspective on the sun

Sylvia Cavanaugh

Day Begins

On North Pier—a jutting assemblage of concrete
and boulders pointing southeast into the open waters
of Lake Michigan and supporting at its tip
a red lighthouse that guides ships into port—

on that pier, early-risers with rods and reels cast lines
into the channel or into open water, sometimes catch
but often do not catch salmon, lake trout, other fish,
while walkers walk, runners run, tourists take
photographs of the lighthouse and of fishing boats
scattered like cake crumbs on a silvery plate.

Small sandpipers dart along the edges pecking tiny
insects, seagulls rest here, mallards swim alongside,
swallows glide and swoop eating lake flies as they go,
and waves tease boulders, nudging and swirling
around and over them or, when organized into
neat rows by passing boats, slapping and slamming.

This morning the sun creeps slowly higher, a kite
on a string, breaks clouds into wisps that dissipate
and cede their space to golden light.

Day gradually speeds up, the hum of cars and trucks
joining gull-squeals, boat-chugs, waves gurgling
and splashing, fishermen's soft voices—
and it's good, all good, this day begun in peace,
in grace and beauty, now fully awake, swinging its arms
and moving freely.

Georgia Ressmeyer

The Bundled Trundler

As we trundle
bundled
fur hat headed
gloved and heavy booted,
scarf layered neck, up to our eyes,
we stumble into snow drifts
whipped by the icy winds
that sting and bite our faces
and frosts our eyelashes,
and that just gets us to
our snow impacted frozen car.
We'll also need to take along
a small pan of hot water to pour over
the frozen door handle, just in case,
then, pray the battery hasn't died overnight.
Is going to work,
getting a newspaper, the mail
or a cappuccino, really worth all this?

Nancy Harrison Durdin

Three

*Wind remakes the land,
and churns the sea. Wings flutter,
sand swirls, we cover our eyes.*

I Need a Storm

Rain falls constant and gentle
washing over me like a prayer,
I open my eyes and scream,
this is not what I need,
not what I must have!

I need
howling gales of wind
violent and unrelenting
slapping my face
biting my cheeks.

I need
rivers rushing
me toward oblivion
pushing me under,
channeling out a new path
through my open chest.

I need
obliteration
of the rotting wound
in my heart.

I need
baptism in chaos
cleansing by rampage
renewal by retribution
devastation never ending.

I need a storm
that meets my rage
head-on!

I need
to fight for my life
and win.

Nancy Harrison Durdin

Honeymoon Cottage in Cedar Key

"Nothing beside remains. Round the decay
Of that colossal wreck, boundless and bare
The lone and level sands stretch far away."

from "Ozymandias" by Percy Bysshe Shelley

Soon it will be nothing—
the honeymoon cottage beside
the shore—its bare remains
subject to the imagination of artists who round
out the stilted skeleton with stories of young lovers, the
bright seascape before the decay.
I too have wondered about them, thought of
the life they must have lived in that
charming cottage by the sea, colossal
skies purple and orange, storms yet to wreck
upon their dreams still as boundless
as their life stretched out before them, and
about them in the cottage, bright and bare,
their naked feet on yellow wood. It was not the
light that drew them, but the water, the sound, lone
and stark, nature's truth. When the first hurricane and
battering waves surprised them and brought them level
with mortality, they felt betrayed by hope. Sunny sands
have forgotten them, as have we who stand and stretch
upon early rising, we vacationing visitors far
from home, we who look once and then away.

Dawn Hogue

Mermaid Tattoo Becomes Enmeshed in Her Relationship

I was crafted carefully and with cunning
to link my ink to this relentless red flow
nailed down to the pulse
like a seashell ocean's echo my
two dimensions bend and arch
they ache to the rhythm of his three as
I'm plastered flat to a twining twitch
of muscle and deeper down
I sense the bone I cannot grasp it makes
my stomach turn and yet my
tiny nipples burn I yearn for him
trapped beneath the death of him
as his outer layer flakes away
and I'm the only witness

we hover over women with
their open legs like rowboat oars
the wretched separation
distantly they beg for us and
gnash their teeth
we heave and sweat
the salty sea and thrash
a flash of scale on
spangled tail
till his eyes roll back
and stare through mine

Sylvia Cavanaugh

Sky View

"That dolphin-torn, that gong-tormented sea"

From "Byzantium," by William Butler Yeats

It was the Cape Cod tidal pool that
taught me I breathe air like the dolphins.
I had believed in my body before it was torn
from the sand floor by a fast rising tide that
tilted back my head in reflexive gasp, gong-
knell filling my brain. Until a man saw my tormented
sky-bound eyes. He saved me from the salt blue sea.

Sylvia Cavanaugh

Down by the Riverside

> "Down by the Riverside, I'm Going to Lay Down
> My Sword and Shield"
>
> —Negro Spiritual

when I was little
I recited
Baghdad, Euphrates, Mesopotamia, Tigris River
and read geography books
that held stories within stories

Once upon a time
a young girl
went down by the riverside
and saw the river turn black
when they emptied the library
and sent books swimming down the Tigris

she believed hope lay in the fish
who maybe could learn to read
or at least live their lives as noble fish
not like human beings
afraid to love
their hearts, their brains

Maryann Hurtt

In 1258, the House of Wisdom library was destroyed during the Mongol invasion of Baghdad along with all the other libraries. It was said the waters of the Tigris ran black for six months with ink from the enormous quantities of books flung into the river. Following the 2003 invasion of Iraq, Iraq's national library and the Islamic library in central Baghdad were burned and destroyed.

Summer Storm

Last night's wind
whomped the weakest
branches from the willow
near the river bank.

Whip switches lie
everywhere, and an
unhealthy impulse
rises in me—I want
to rake it all up
and make neat
this nature's chaos.

But instead, my dog
and I tread across the
litter, as do splay-footed
geese and tottering robins
unearthing worms. Insects
will devour the rot of
what remains.

Slender-leafed branches
will float for a time upon
the water before sinking
and bubbling into muck.

And though we face our
own storms with stoic posture,
defying the inevitable,
we all go down
to carbon
in the end.

Dawn Hogue

Sea Levels Rising

When Lake Michigan climbs the bluff
claws her way up up up past riprap
dropped to stabilize the bank she
clutches weeds saplings the trunks of
trees hauls her dripping body to the top
stops to admire the view from an
Adirondack chair in someone's yard
moves into a mansion for a brief respite
swims in the indoor pool with zebra
mussels still clinging to her green
algae-tangled hair sleeps in a queen-
size bed surrounded by windows that
crack from the roar of her outsize snore
tries to make a fire but can't find
a dry match finally gives up bursts
through the front door rushes across
the lawn to the street where she flows
gradually west seeps into every home
liberates tropical fish gushes up a slope
until she comes to a single-story flat-
roofed house almost square in shape
which she lifts from its foundation
and tows like a toy in her wake while
an old woman sits inside at a small desk
pen in hand sifting her brain for
something remarkable to recount to her
sister in a nursing home six states away
not even noticing a change in the view
though she does feel a bit more adrift
than usual and can't help wishing
something extraordinary would happen
to make her letter more exciting but
so far nothing has and she doubts it will

Georgia Ressmeyer

Back to "Mothers' Waters"

He burst forth from my womb,
gasping,
soaking wet,
and fighting.

Freed from
the sea of life
that had nurtured
and sustained him.

Tears drowned my face;
I cried with joy,
my son, my boy!

In far too short, and
precious time;
the sky turned black,
and hurled him back
into "Mother's waters."

He was gasping,
soaking wet, and
surely fighting for his life.

This time
"Mother's" watery embrace
sustained him not.

Tears flooded my face,
I cried, he's died, he's died,
in "Mother's waters."

Nancy Harrison Durdin

The river is insulted

Lazy you have called me,
winding, as if I have no
aim in life, no purpose but
to flow from here to there.
But you have seen my
raging rapids, called me
whitewater, called me
swollen and angry.
You have seen me boil
over mossy rocks
and surge against
the shore.
I am
no
more
the simple river
you picnic by, and dare
to dip your toes into. I am the
maker of gullies and the shaper of land.
I am the sailor of debris and rocks and you
are right to be in awe as you move to higher ground.

Dawn Hogue

The River's Rising and Other Important Things

Early one morning, I received a call from
an elderly friend about water rising up to her
back door in her little home in Black River.
I called a mutual friend and we quickly drove
to her home, boots in hand, to help her
evacuate if needed. We sat helpless
in her kitchen, while we looked out her window.
Watching as the water rose up to her back door,
she suddenly pointed, shouting, "look, look"!
Jumping up, expecting the worst, only to
hear her say, "it's a red tanager"!
Joyfully, we hugged each other and laughed.
My friend and I had seen only impending disaster,
she saw a red tanager, and opened her heart to it,
showing us that the human spirit can celebrate
beauty in the throes of impending disaster;
and thereby survive it.

Nancy Harrison Durdin

Alligator Log

Alligator log, your two eyes lie just above the water's surface,
the river lapping over your barky back, coloring you black.
Your presence does not alarm the geese who flat foot it
up the slope to the school nearby. Nothing bothers them,
those intrusive squatters who have no sense of decency.

Downstream, you may be interested to know, a pair of
Great White Egrets has laid five eggs, while you dine
on the soggy droppings of a willow tree. Further down
is the Mill Pond, where fish live undisturbed, for the
Angler's platform the city built goes unused.

I also am not alarmed by the fact that you linger
day to day so closely to the path where I walk. I respect
your right to be just where you are, unlike the discarded
milk carton and sodden cardboard box and their cousin,
a rusty bedframe that lies half submerged in muck.

Dawn Hogue

My Repugnant Tar Creek Orange Self

Miami, Oklahoma April 2, 2016

I see folks stare
right into my orange self
like I'm some kind of repugnant
aberration
wonder what they see
reflection, maybe?
always understood whatever we do
to each other
comes right back
maybe even tenfold
folks might think about that
when they let life
carry on just like nothing
they do or can do
makes much difference
maybe, just maybe when we really see each other
for what we are and could be
someone will wake up, call the alarm
find the power to do something
before it's too late

Maryann Hurtt

Tar Creek in northeastern Oklahoma, southeastern Kansas is the site of what has been called "the worst environmental disaster no one has ever heard of." Lead and zinc mining took place here from the 1800s till the early 70s. Most of the lead for American ammunition during World War I and II came from these mines. The water in Tar Creek is now orange.

Rain on a Tuesday Afternoon Amidst a Drought

Silvery torrents of rain slide
down the window pane
bouncing high as they hit
the parched earth.
Pounding down
against the hardscrabble ground
demanding to be let in,
drawn down,
absorbed,
before being lost forever
to the greedy wind.
Suddenly the earth softens,
swallowing a refreshing throatfull,
with glee and gratitude.
Finally sated after months of thirst
shouting through moistened lips:
"Hallelujah!"

Nancy Harrison Durdin

Sheboygan Marsh 6 a.m.

the marsh smokes
this just start of day
the yellow yolk sun
sneaks through the trees
and I sit almost silent
my arm makes an arc
bait and line slide
through ghost vapor air

just to feel the tug
of a creature I can't see
is enough
when air, water
fish, humans share
this dewy drenched world
full of possibility

Maryann Hurtt

Water When the Wind Blows

When we look at our ramshackle farm now,
and what we called our "Eiffel Tower" as kids,
memories and tears begin to flow.

When the wind blew the windmill blades
turned, and the water ran down the
rusty old pump, delivering water to us,
sometimes even overflowing the tank.

However, on too many quiet windless days,
we would be hand pumping the water;
maximum effort, minimal results.

While we had enough water we survived,
without enough, we lost the farm,
the land, and the way of life we struggled
so hard, for so long, to preserve.

When small family farms are lost,
we have all lost something very valuable,
and we are all the poorer for it.

Nancy Harrison Durdin

Bergie Bits

Thousands of white pupils
bulge skyward in blue-grey eye pools,
bob-float the waters of the Amalia Glacier.
They vibrate ripples of lesser vision
than their stalwart valley mother seer
on shore.
These iceberg bits, born as calves,
No longer nurse or moo.
They fizzle cold salt,
cavort our wake,
somersault the sea.

Marilyn Zelke Windau

Existential Rain

Thick gray clouds
spill their contents
long silver drops
of cool liquid
glisten like mercury
sliding down
the window pane.
What is its destiny,
plunging itself into
the hungry, parched earth;
providing life itself,
saving lives?
Or is it just caught up in the
chaos and crisis of the moment
on its way down,
not knowing its meaning or end,
aware of no purpose at all,
or who's behind it;
Is it just an existential wash?

Nancy Harrison Durdin

There Was This Original Me

The original me
on a September morning
pushed my feet
into red rain boots
each with a single red button.
I opened my new umbrella
for the long walk to school,
alone and complete in the cold
pelt of raindrops.
Gray rivers gushed along gutters
I navigated.

A thin silver stem
rose from the hooked handle
to unfold into a complicated
metal frame, delicate
and elegant as an Eiffel Tower
I could hold in one hand.
A silken dome
stretched wide as the sky overhead.
Its opulent color
drenched down and around me,
backlit by gossamer sun

I had chosen the design
at a store
with my mother.
We opened it once
in sacred ceremony
on a glaring August day.

Sylvia Cavanaugh

The Opportunist

The rain poured,
the lightning struck
the power out,
a frog sitting on
a piece of an old picket fence
floats by in a puddle of water
on the floor of the barn.
All he needs now is a
tiny white sail, and
his journey could
get really interesting.
Carpe Diem, dear green frog,
bon voyage, and pray for rain!

Nancy Harrison Durdin

Naucrate

Ever the mother of Icarus
my name means power of the sea
but with no edge of my own
my boundaries are defined
by other bodies
I've conformed to the contours
of my children
their dreams and sadnesses
I've soothed and cooled
the anger
sometimes flaring hot
between disparate particles
I'm the participle
that describes nouns
a verb downgraded
to an adjective
I'm the swelling tide
my thoughts are salt
a brine brim full
on the brink of saturation
I might have held him afloat

Sylvia Cavanaugh

Four

*Spirit mist rises
at dawn, the sea shore awash
in light, dolphins breach.*

In Memoriam

Renate Ruth Gabriella Klein
March 31, 1981 - September 14, 2016

We lost you to a rogue wave,
a metastatic cancer.

You wore your water wings,
your vest, were wrenched
away from us too fast.

We waited on the shore
and sank,
are sinking yet.

Saltwater gave you buoyancy
you didn't have on land.

It held you up, let you walk
along the ocean floor.

Now I look for you
each time I crest a wave,
hoping to find you
in the trough,
where we can race.

You won't need water wings,
may wear the other kind.

You have already
won the race.

Georgia Ressmeyer

every poem

I have ever written
begins right here
at this river
where grandmother and mother slip
down the rocks
to bend, squat, see
really see
these pebbles, this cold
cold water
and I tiptoe into the rush
of it all
knowing this is where
I belong
and how sixty years
will pass
but one tiny breath
of river
will carry me
forever

Maryann Hurtt

Ahab and the Whale

"How can those terrified vague fingers push/The feathered glory from her loosening thighs?"

From "Leda and the Swan," William Butler Yeats

Sudden slip along the tilted wet wood of a whaleboat, how
his legs flew unbidden skyward. Can
this treachery ever seem anything but slow motion in memory? Those
white moments felt from the depth of bowels; his youthful mind terrified.
A whaling life was once just the vague
fancy of a bored schoolboy, counting days on his fingers.
Figures of any kind were not his thing. O, how Father would push.
But no, he was destined to stride across a boat careening atop the
viscous roll of salt-gray oblivion. To be almost feathered
in confidence; to command water. The glory
of a two-legged beast, with lungs, to lord over seas; a glory derived from
the delusion of dominion over fishes. The sleek ship; her
oily industry; all this promise before that endless loosening
grip. Before twin rows of rounded teeth ground to marrow all bone below the thigh.

Sylvia Cavanaugh

Evening Comes to Vernazza

inspired by the art quilt "View of Vernazza" by Pat Bishop

Evening descends slowly
upon ancient bleached stone.
Sun casts pink into blue
onto long narrow window glass.
Inside pink and gold glasses
tink in toasts, voices chatter
indistinct harmony.
Golden wires glow in teardrop bulbs
suspended overhead in crystal.
An open-window breeze
blows warm and salty.
We breathe deeply.
Below us, water moves
at its own pace to the sea,
controlled by greater whims
of tide and moon.

Dawn Hogue

Beach Picnic

I've been planning a picnic at the beach
although still too chill
I long for soaring seagull cry
tilted rainbow umbrellas
cotton towels on hot sand
cold water you get used to over dares
I want to reinforce this rite
with my almost grown children
before they disperse

I remember the old folks
in the mountains
they grew vegetables and gourds
gave me nickels
or sometimes pennies
with Indian heads and oak wreaths
from the top drawer of a dark dresser
I wonder if they knew how unknown
they were to become
just a few decades after easing
into the swell
of their own sloping ground

Sylvia Cavanaugh

Water Wolf

the pike
I pull out of the ice
flop-flips its gold
speckled weight
straight oxygen assaults
his gills
dagger tooth incisors open-close
you push-pull the hook
and behold his water wolf majesty

to be so near
is to bow
in honor and awe

you slide his body
through the circle of cleared ice
a few twists and he is gone
back to home sweet
water home
where he is king
and we are humble servants

Maryann Hurtt

I Dream in Water

To be able to unlock oxygen
ease it from the water
tease it through scarlet gills

they say my eyes are like water
that a mirror
or sometimes glass
resembles a deepened pool
just wishful reflections
projections of desire

O, to be held aloft
gently
adrift in viscous sediment float
beginnings of eons
fragmentary flora floating
and photosynthesizing
above a sandy sifting floor

how I hate the rocky dry
of land
air too thin to dream

Sylvia Cavanaugh

Deer on the Kohler Andrae Crestline

Slowly, slowly Lake Michigan opens
I walk between waves and the crestline,
those hills of sand scrubbed by sprawling,
earth-hugging evergreens.
Cold are the lake waters of January.
Ice pockmarks blemish the skin of shore.
Above the waving, white hair
of dry beach grasses, deer stand.
Silhouetted sentinels,
they guard the winter silence.
Straight backed, necks erect,
they raise their racks as antennae.
Snorting softly at the sound
of ice glass shattering,
of broken icicles tinkling tunes
on the shoreline, they turn,
hoof-tap snow,
continue their guardian march.

Marilyn Zelke Windau

Empty Nest

I live in your breeding area, it seems, and this week I have observed you at the nest your mate built for you at the base of a sloping lawn on the river's eastern shore, a long grassy hill fringed in willow trees, where he found a tangle of fallen branches to be perfect protection for your eggs, those bluish green vessels for your chicks that you and he will nurture for six weeks on the regurgitated river life you find nearby. When snowflakes start their seasonal descent, a few here, a few there, before they begin their onslaught, before they bury us in our own nests, you will leave this shore, flap your powerful wings, and propel yourself two wing beats per second southward, perhaps to other brackish waters, or to a tidal flat, sandy silt, teeming with fiddler crabs. Before your journey, will you talk with your chicks? Will you prepare them for the grueling flight ahead, advise them on how to buck the strong winds you've learned over time to manage? Or do you acknowledge that in life we must all find our own way, that even the inevitability of leaving one's parents is something we must do alone, without direction, map or otherwise.

Dawn Hogue

Candle Waxes — Love Wanes

candle weeps wax
lover drifts into slumber
eyes watch, and weep rivers

Nancy Harrison Durdin

On the Menu

The river gouged its banks
to offer stronger coffee.

Trails were chomped on and
narrowed like crullers.

Trees that had been toppled
for stir-sticks lay useless
still rooted in fast-moving java.

Cow-parsnip waiters with
white plates on their heads
danced between pillars
in dining-room woods

where fragrant Dame's Rocket
and Tall Meadow Rue reclined
on their stems while their roots
sipped espresso.

Wild roses trembled at riverside
tables as I hurried past
in mud-plastered boots, careful
not to slip off the path into
fast-moving mocha

where I might dissolve
like a spoonful of sugar.

Georgia Ressmeyer

River Mistress

my father has a mistress
she spills secrets
he absorbs with ears wide open
old hands caress crevices
she allows passage to her treacherous body
and they dance in light

soon he will be salmon

Maryann Hurtt

Letter to Lorine

    Wisconsin poet Lorine Niedecker (1903-1970)
    lived much of her life near the flooding Rock River

Lorine your little
    house
        no wonder
you wrote
    short

no more than tiny
    paper
        scraps
fit
    pocket

house as Rock
    rose —
rock
    paper
        scissors

floods of words
    to pocket
        trickles
scissors cut
    paper

paper covered
    Rock
paper won—
    words rowed
        out

Georgia Ressmeyer

Trinity

I sit shivering
in my father's drift boat
the sun has not found its way
over the Cascades
the man I spent my first eighteen years
waits next to me
he's 92 now
still rises when it's dark
loves these invisible salmon
like brothers
my husband pushes-pulls oars
through mountain cold McKenzie water
we cast lines
ponder fish journeys
to eat what has worked so hard
feels like communion
the river, my prayer

Maryann Hurtt

Dragonflies

facing west
a squadron
ready to deploy
warming wings
sunny lake dock

thunder bugs
drab armor
concealing lace
jeweled eyes
summer's angels

outstretched hand
landing spot
not a thing to fear
insect light
we are but one

Dawn Hogue

River in the Sea

South of the Falkland Islands

Within the undulating
sway grass-bound banks,
the sea shivers its current forward,
widens to the horizon's plates
where cumulus accumulates.
Reflected light security-blankets
a hidden populace of icefish,
of dolphin, of whales.
Deep on the Antarctic storage shelf
rocks are silent.
Salt murmurs the water,
quieting icemaker desires.
Glitter funnels toward me,
spews shine,
sparkle dust.

Marilyn Zelke Windau

Cottage Summer

Early summer is a cottage dweller
arriving with a carload of clutter,
breezing in as if to stay forever,
as if pleasure were all that mattered,
barefoot or sandaled, prone to be prone
in bed, on sand, in hammock, on water,
reclining and reading or napping,
fishing, sailing, drifting, as careless
of time as the moon lolling in a firefly sky,
sleepy, relaxed, slack and stretched out,
poked by mosquitoes and rippling waves,
ogling fireworks, lightning and thunder-works,
barely conscious of days sliding by,
of all that cannot last, of time slipping past.

Georgia Ressmeyer

How Nancy Drew Learned to Fish

if you learn stillness
the mucky pond
shares fish secrets
you become a detective
of smells and faint tugs
they bring you
eye to eye
with creatures
alien
from your vertical life
gifts
from the depths
mysteries to love

Maryann Hurtt

Acknowledgements

The Grand Avenue Poetry Collective would like the thank the editors of following publications in which these poems first appeared, some in slightly different form:

The Lyric: "Pristine Joy"

Peninsula Pulse: "Daedalus Surfs Refugio Beach"

Wisconsin DNR Calendar (Wisconsin DNR, 2012): "Comfort"

An Ariel Anthology: Transformational Poetry and Art, 2015 (Ariel Woods Books, 2015). "On the Beach at Daybreak"

Blue Heron Review. "Great Lake Lullaby"

Staring Through My Eyes (Finishing Line Press, 2016). "Rope Climb"

The Journey II: "Icarus Was My Brother"

Stoneboat Literary Journal: "Beach Glass"

Wisconsin Fellowship of Poets' Calendar, 2014: "Water Looking Up"

Verse Wisconsin: "Midsummer, 1961"

Wisconsin Fellowship of Poets Museletter: "Dance of the Pigeon River"

Peninsula Poets: "Mermaid Tattoo Becomes Enmeshed in Her Relationship"

Silver Birch Press Poetry and Prose Series: "Sky View"

Seems: "Sea Levels Rising"

Wisconsin Fellowship of Poets' Calendar 2017: "Sheboygan Marsh 6 a.m."

Intersections: Art & Poetry (Sheboygan Visual Artists, 2016): "Water When the Wind Blows"